masala

chai

alyees qureshi

|| gup shup ||

I still remember the day that I decided on the title
masala chai.
It was so seamless.
I was lounged in my apartment writing poems
after just having made a hot cup of chai.
I could hear my heart whispering for me to dive even
deeper into my soul with my writing.
It ached to explore the other half of me
that I had always suppressed.

And so I began writing what would unknowingly
become the first poem for this book.
With a cup of chai sitting on the table,
I realized that masala chai was the perfect metaphor
for not only a poem, or even this book,
but my life as a whole.
I am an entire recipe of rich experiences and memories
that have led me to become the man that I am today.

In that moment I reminisced the times as a child
when my mother would leave half a cup of chai
on the stove for me before she left for work.
Every morning in that empty house I would microwave
that cup and dunk cake rusk in it until it broke off.

I couldn't believe that I had ever forgotten
that simplest memory when it was so innate.
The only reason that I even know how to make chai,
is because I watched my mother make it
countless times growing up.

Chai was the only thing that my father would ever ask
me to make, and it was the perfect remedy that my
grandmother would offer me everytime I got sick.

And like an epiphany, I finally understood why I was
always so meticulous in the way that I made chai.
Because it has become such a cherished constant
throughout my life, that it has to be done right
every single time that it's made.

———

Entering young adulthood and living on my own,
I gained a new sense of freedom.
And part of that freedom, was abandoning home.
Although I hadn't made a pot of chai in years,
suddenly a spark to begin again
and experiment with new spices overtook me.

I found myself mixing a cauldron of chai
and every spice you could name.
I was finally making use of all those Desi spices shoved
in the back of my pantry that my mother had given me.
And as the aromas overcame me,
it triggered the memories of when my father and I
used to brew masala chai together when I was so young.

And that was when I finally realized
that my heart ached for the smell again because it
yearned to return home.
I was so homesick that I never wanted to admit it,
until now.

———

I never expected my extravagant chai recipe
to become so well known among my friends and family.
Famed for being the perfect blend of spices
and with just the right amount of sweetness and cream.
Friends would come over after a long day of class
or dance practice, just to gup shup the night away
over a cup of my chai.
I mean, people will always listen
to what you have to say
if you offer them a good cup of chai.

And so, I suggest taking a look at my recipe on the last
page and brewing yourself a cup before you embark on
my poetic journey with me.
I wish I could brew and pour out a mug for you
by my own hand.
But for now,
this recipe is the closest level of intimacy we can reach.
Drink it one sip at a time, as it may be the first time you
have had a wholesome cup of authentic chai.
And if it's not your first time,
then let it just immerse you in the feeling of home.

———

At an early point in my life,
the effects of discrimination and being a minority in
America really started to take an effect on me.
And to be honest,
I never even noticed until I began to write this book.
The more I wrote,
the more aware I became of how
I had always been an outsider,
when all I wanted was to be on the inside.

In fact, I grew so ashamed of my culture
that I went to great lengths to hide it.
Sadly, I know that many like me can relate to
this helpless and hopeless feeling too.

Fortunately however,
as a young adult I started to realize
how tasteless the façade of fitting in was.
I missed the richness of desi culture.
I missed having casual conversations
with my parents over dinner.
I missed being true to myself and living genuinely with
the people that would love and care for me the most.
I missed making chai with my family.

And so from then on it became my own personal
mission to come back home.
I started watching Bollywood movies again
to improve my Urdu,
I started a bhangra team to perform at festivals,
And I finally began to admit my love for daal chawal,
haleem, nihari, biryani, samosas and butter chicken.
I mean who cares about the ghee
when it tastes so damn good.
But most importantly,
I perfected my own personal recipe for masala chai.

————

That's probably why a part of me dies whenever I go
to a coffee shop and hear someone order
a masala chai tea latte.
Because I know full well that they are getting scammed.
Or when I go to a grocery store and see cartons of

masala chai tea concentrate on the racks,
I honestly cringe at the level of injustice for chai.
Especially when someone tells me that they hate chai
and I'm like okay where did you try it from?
and they state one or both of the previously
aforementioned scenarios,
I die.

And it's not like I don't give the local coffee shop
a fair chance,
I do.
I pay the five dollars for my overpriced cup of
concentrate chai knowing that I'm going to regret it.
And I hope that just maybe this place is going to be
the one to get it right. But no.
I take that first sip, and I die.
It's just not the same.

There are no shortcuts or concentrates
that will give you its truest taste.
If something isn't your cup of tea,
then at least make sure it was brewed right
and then try a second cup.
Anything you do in life,
you always want to give it its fairest chance
before you walk away from it.
That means taking the time to do it right,
not expecting it to be done right for you.

———

And so this book was born the very moment when I had
written that first poem back in my humble apartment:
masala chai.

And from that day forward
my writing had drastically changed.
Suddenly I was able to tap into my heart for emotions
and memories that I had previously suppressed.
The poems did not and would not stop flowing,
as if I had unlocked some next level chakra.

Maybe that's why I feel so at peace
to finally have my book enter into this world.
After five years of hesitation, writing, and dedication.
You are now holding the very fiber of my being
within your hands.

———

I wanted to create this book as an entire world
of imagery, language, and culture.
It was my own method of absorbing my culture
and translating it into terms that I knew.
I write to learn and improve my understanding
of the world around me.

If I could write poetry in Urdu, I absolutely would have.
But instead my present skills limit my writing to only
titles in Urdu and poems in English.
This was my attempt at bridging the beauty of the Urdu
language into words that I am able to express.

I designed this journey as a metaphorical recipe
for finding the inner values of yourself,
in and out of love.
Starting off as young love and moving onto heartbreak
all while suffering the loss of home,
and finally ending with the realization of self love.

The metaphorical recipe is as follows:

Bloom. You can't start a cup of tea until the earth gives you the ingredients to do so.
This chapter is romantic, new, and blossoming.
Embodying the purity, innocence, and naïvety in love.

Waves. There is no tea without water.
I wanted to show how love has highs and lows in the same way that water does too.
The story of *Waves* starts out as ice that melts into water which then rises again as steam.
Look closely because even within those three states, are its own highs and lows,
because water is always flowing.
This chapter is one of my favorites because I really enjoyed writing as if i was a waterbender.

Heat is the sudden spark of excitement when you meet that someone special.
The lust, the passion, the intensity, the tender warmth, but also the burning.
A flame is unpredictible and so is this chapter.

Boil is heartbreak.
Whether from the suffering of unrequited love or unfaithfulness, it portrays confusion.
And is turbulent just like rolling, boiling water.
In the same way that one may leave their emotions bottled up, at some point they do resurface and need release too.

Brew is finding your way back home.
This chapter begins with my simplest memories of
home, but throughout are the woes I have against
discrimination and trying to find acceptance too.
Likewise are the discords that I have with Desi culture,
because it is not perfect either.
I hope that many will be able to relate
or even simply grow from this chapter.

Strain is the purification of the soul.
For so long throughout this journey you have suffered
the greivances and sorrows of heartbreak.
But it is important to rid yourself of those impurities
and finally begin healing.
This chapter is about rising,
and learning to love one's self after much suffering.

Savor. The chai has been made, the soul has been healed,
and now it is time to finally sit back
and reflect on the experiences of your journey:
the good and the bad.
Many images I used throughout this book I reuse here
to tie any loose ends back together.
This chapter is using your new found strength to help
and guide others.

I can tell that my chai is getting cold
when malai starts to form at the surface.
So pinkies out, let's sip our tea
and begin our journey together!

– alyees qureshi

|| khandan ||

to my mother who was my first home,
and for the lengths you took
to bring me into this world.

to my father who taught me
the values of becoming a man.

to my brothers who beared the burdens
of being the strongest.

to my dear sisters who taught me,
how to respect and love
a woman in this world.

thank you for supporting me,
when it was not easy.

———

|| dostana ||

to the friends who listened
with not their ears
but their hearts,
thank you.

|| intangible ||

to the soul who touched me
and fused with mine,
we are now intangible,
for we are always ours.

contents

bloom – love

waves – states

heat – fire

boil – chaos

brew – culture

strain – purify

savor – home

young love grows
like a blossoming flower.
each fragrance, its own story.

|| chrysalises ||

chyrsalises hang inside me
destined to bloom upon your touch.
that must be why
i get butterflies in my stomach
each time my name
spills from your lips
like silk and nectar.

|| titli ||

fluttering, a butterfly has taken flight.
entranced in your iridescent aroma,
it follows your fragrant breath
that is sweet like nectar.

never lingering upon a flower for too long,
it softly dances.
every stroke of its wings
carries a humming heartbeat.

traveling far away, resisting return,
an untamed butterfly kisses the sky.
fluttering, my heart has taken flight.

|| two lips ||

tulips touch to make new life,
two lips touch to make new love,
new love too becomes new life.

|| tongue tied ||

let's tie our tongues together,
like the tides,
until our lips
can knot
keep up.

|| intoxicated ||

i was intoxicated
not by your beauty
but by your mind.

although i don't mind the beauty.

|| mine ||

your beauty blew my mind
like a triggered land mine.
and whence the rubble finally settled,
i discovered a mine full of jewels
inside your mind,
that could for once,
read mine.

|| jasmine ||

everyone chases after you,
for your aroma is intoxicating,
and your beauty is striking.
your hair overflows
like the blossoming vines
that overhang across my trellis.
yet your vines are strong and vibrant,
for you climb even higher
than my gaze can meet.

your nectar drips from paradise,
like the blossoms of a jasmine.
one sip and i haven fallen in love
within the tangles of your vines.
tied with you, i too bloom as you do.

|| hold her ||

they say love is blind
and lovers cannot see
yet beauty is in the eye of the beholder,
and all i want to do is hold her.

|| fields ||

a field of dry wheat
may not appear lush gold
until a field of lavender
gently flourishes beside it.

|| autumn ||

leaves only fall in autumn
as they fall in love with you.
i am of those leaves.

|| queen of the night ||

i spent a lifetime alone
stranded like a cactus.
my skin was prickly,
and no one ever dared to draw near.
out of fear of being pricked,
or rather i was unworthy to be near.
and although i was home,
for years i felt lost.

but then bloomed a single flower
who offered me solace
during the frigid nighttime.
her fragrance was foreign,
and her glowing white petals
lit the desert darkness so brightly,
that i feared to go blind.

and although she soon hid
from the sweltering daytime,
in that one night,
i was able to bear the fruits of my sadness
and return to the earth in solemn.

|| siren ||

your words are soft like the dancing of rain.
from you i have the world to gain.
your smile brightens the depths of the sea,
the worlds, the universe, eternity.

to imagine your beauty, i never dare.
this unworthy mind, to you unfair.
hold my hand, explore and see,
the echoing depths of the seven seas.

you are the beacon of light that i call home.
of that i am sure, i have always known.
through the tempest you keep me calm,
like a siren, i follow your song.

|| palms ||

i traced the lines
within the palms of your hands
with my fingertips.
and like braille,
i mapped them within my mind,
to find my way back home.

and past the palms in the sands
and with the wind's command,
i discovered a new homeland,
within the palms of your hands.

|| footsteps ||

sunrise until sunset
i listened to your footsteps.
winds guiding my path
my sail leads me to you.

you who knows no path,
lost and searching for meaning,
my arms extend to you.
hugging you as the shore does the sea.

and as the storm ceases,
sun splitting the night,
soft sunbeams burst
and illuminate the world.
the world that is ours.

|| atlas ||

atlas,
you are omniscient.
you draw the stars,
you guide the tides,
and in your pages i confide.
thus with your infinite scope,
and you as my compass,
i know, i can endure the globe.

|| stories ||

i am the ink
that follows the feather,
you are the quill
that pierces the paper.
together we write stories.

|| lightning ||

you are the bolt of lightning
that strikes the sky
and stuns even the sun.
i am the thunder that shadows.

|| flourish ||

uncanny is it,
that the sun lies perfectly with the earth,
just enough to make her flourish.

|| constellation ||

i drew a line
to connect the stars
and the stars aligned with you.
and so with you i gazed.

|| worlds ||

some worlds
have stronger pulls than others.
but the only world that matters
in all the galaxies
and in every universe,
is the one with you.

|| dimensions ||

my heart was made of four walls,
like a dark room.
until you managed to break
the fourth wall,
and light flooded my veins,
casting a shadow
that had more dimensions
than even i had ever known.

|| moonlight ||

moonlight spills forth from your face
like honey dripping from its catacombs.
milkier than the moon at its fullest,
droplets dew upon your face
as they pool into my hands.
sweet and wholesome
i long to taste your beauty
that drips of milk and honey.

(inspired by rupi kaur)

|| magnets ||

i can't explain why i feel
like the stars are aligning.
that every spark in the universe
twist and turned
in our direction
just to watch us find each other.
it's as if the stars flipped
two repelling magnets
that ache to become whole.
not knowing that their other half
lies on opposite poles of the earth.
and so my body pulls to you
like a current of lightning
searching for a home.
it soars to you through the winds,
defiant of gravity,
in the same cosmic attraction
as magnets do.

|| jannat ||

remain as you are
for the sky herself sighs at your beauty,
and lies at your feet.
even jannat herself trembles to hold you.

|| azaan ||

you are the rain that the soil cries for
during the summer.
you are the rosiness painted across my face
amongst the snow.
you are the peaceful melody
that soothes my ears at dawn.
you are the harmonies
that the birds sing along to the azaan.
all life awakens upon your call.
the rain, the earth, the birds, my blood.

and yes,
you are even the somberness
that palls upon our faces at dusk,
for we are sent to slumber.
but fear not.
for we do see your return in our dreams.
and when we awaken
to your call to prayer,
as the sun rises once again
upon your name.

|| tasbih ||

how envious i am of the tasbih
that knows every fingerprint
upon your troubled hands!
share your prayers with me
as i pass through your fingertips
countless times,
so that i can be the one
to ease your sorrows
and soften your gentle hands
once again.

|| mehndi ||

i cannot wait for the day
to hold your hands
and find my name
hidden within the intricacies
of your mehndi.

|| mayoun ||

as naariyal ki tael soaks my hair,
and slicks across my forehead,
i gaze as jasmines are braided
within your hair.
together our aromas fill me with dreams
of our new home that awaits us.

and while your palms lay open
upon mine as your mehndi dries,
let me dab them with nimbu cheeni
and feed you mitai by my own hand.

let me lather your already glowing skin
in haldi that is so fluid like gold.
i want to shower you in riches forever,
so that you always smile
so auspiciously
like on this day.

|| ayaat ||

again and again
i read your name like an ayaat
as to never forget the curves of each letter
or the strains of each word.
because i found that
tracing your name with just my fingertips
and whispering your name under my breath,
was the only way that i found sukoon.

|| du'a ||

let me hold you
like a du'a,
and never let go.

|| darcheeni ||

yes my skin is milk
and your bark is cinnamon.
we are told not to mix,
but together we are simply
sugar and spice.
a flavor that even you
cannot resist.

|| sugarcanes ||

your juices drip from sugarcanes
and they alone
are sweet enough to taste.
but everyone wants to refine you,
bleach you into a color that you are not.
but i promise you my love,
you are sweeter
than raw sugar alone.

|| masala chai ||

i want to embrace you
in the way that milk
fuses with chai.
bleeding into a single rich color.
for you are the jaggery
that sweetens the tongue
and soothes my sharpness.
you are the masala that stirs trouble,
depth, and flavor into my world.
you are the malai that blankets me
in gentle warmth.
and the rusk that is dipped
and soaks my love with eternal compassion.
i yearn to be the earthen teacup
that hugs and holds you together
when you have no place else to flow.

|| gulabi chai ||

the token of love is a rose,
and yet it only wilts away into the past
as you idly admire it from afar.

thus when i give you a rose,
you must pluck its petals
and tear them apart;
scatter them in rapid waters
to extract the very essence of not the rose
but my love in potency.

you must enrichen it with dhood,
garnish it with pistas and badam,
and savor every sip
as you take it into your body
and absorb it.
only then will we have attained
the highest level of intimacy.

|| laal ||

paint me red,
naked red.
no more twisting and turning,
just paint me in the color of your love,
with the blood that runs through your veins.
with your darkest red.
deeper and denser.
only *your* red.

my heart is fragile like glass
even the slightest nazar can break it
and with it, if you slit my skin
i would pour red,
only *your* red.

dancing through the tips of my fingers
i would part your hair in vermillion
and paint you in *my* red.
until you are dripping in *one* red.
only *our* red.

|| saffron ||

we are rarer than honey,
for our dyes create gold alone.
tongues ache to taste
the sweet and spice
of the very threads of saffron
that tie us together.

كهسمش

love is not constant,
it flows like waves.

|| tundra ||

even across the barren tundra,
life finds a way to grow.
i am the arctic moss,
who clings upon the rocks and snow.

|| frost ||

winter is coming,
and so the fearful leaves fall.
but it is the leaves that stay,
and endure the frost
who are strong enough
to provide for the tree.

|| firn ||

as remnant snow is soon forgotten,
it becomes impenetrable.
yet through the wet sugar,
a growing fern frond struggles to unfurl.
i too unfurl my arms towards you
through the blizzard
to keep you warm within the firn.

|| frozen ||

you are viscous like water,
spilling over the edges,
and seeping through the cracks.
but clever as you pool
into every crevice of the earth.

yet once the earth absorbs you,
and you dissipate into the air,
i would never see your return.

and so i will hold you even tighter,
to freeze this very moment.
because when atoms get cold,
they nestle together for warmth,
so tightly until they are frozen solid.

|| fjords ||

even ice can flow,
for the fjords were carved by glaciers.
we must move as them,
flowing slowly forward,
as only they could afford to do so.

|| avalanche ||

peaks and valleys,
i have been both.
valleys so low,
that the ocean has drowned me.

but with you,
i have seen peaks so high,
so unconquerable,
that i have been submerged
under an ocean of snow.
this icy ocean that i hug so tightly,
so that you never slip and slide
along the treacherous mountainside.
rolling and tumbling,
as loosening snow,
until you crash into the ocean,
and melt away with its flow.

|| noon dab ||

the ice that grows between us
spreads distance
yet keeps us still.

dip your hand in salt,
but spill it not,
and promise to never
melt the ice with it.
for taking even
a grain of salt to the ice
will shatter the silence
that keeps us still.

|| comet ||

oh my love from the stars above,
as much heat as there is in space,
there is even more ice.
if you are lost and frozen,
enter my orbit,
and collide into my arms.
split into two if you must.
and as people wish upon
your unraveling tails,
i will absorb your impact.

|| snowflake ||

glinting across the sunlight,
as you gently fall from the sky,
you find home within my numbing hands.
precious and fragile,
you melt from the warmth of my palms,
pooling within the thin lines,
before i can even taste it.
my tears join you in our sorrow.

|| hail ||

the sky wept in hail,
aching to be soothed.
and so i hailed for the sun,
who in turn haled the snow.

|| h2o ||

i am the hydrogen,
that is lost in two pieces,
volatile and untamed.
but you are the oxygen,
that has bonded to me
and has given me fluidity.
together,
we are the universal solvents of life.

alyees qureshi

|| water ||

and still they search
for planets that bear us.
for we are unattainable
like water.

|| kizuna ||

could it be?
that the very water that falls from my sky,
was once the same water
that flowed through your river?
that the very water i have tasted,
has once crossed your mouth too?

it could be
that our paths have weaved,
unraveled,
and intertwined once again,
becoming one single thread.
that a cosmic knot binds our souls together,
my body having been your body.
even if no two snowflakes are alike,
the water they are molded from are of the same.

yes. it must be
that the water that nourishes me,
and quenches your thirst;
that enters our bodies as we absorb it,
is one of the same flow.

|| estuary ||

my emotions flow like a river,
it twists and turns
like a serpent.
the river is rapid,
it storms and torrents,
and from my heart,
it empties into the estuary
that is your hands.
do not spill a drop.

|| waterfalls ||

i want to fall in love with you
in the way that water falls for the earth.
pouring even when the river
spills over the edge.
crashing into the hands of the earth
who eagerly waits to hold me below.

|| erupt ||

how do you erupt geysers
from my skin
with just your touch alone.
you pour rivers from within me
that even i never knew were running.

|| safe ||

i feel safe knowing,
that you are not going anywhere.
that the water is still,
and the tides are unchanging.
that at this very moment in time,
and at this point in space,
the person that you want to be with,
is me.

|| water lily ||

water lily,
you float freely through the pond,
you ripple as it stirs,
and bloom as you please.
yet still you stay anchored to the pond,
and never sink.

you have commanded the waters
long before i have.

|| baans ||

i am the bamboo
that holds the earth together,
and secures it from erosion.
my roots expand as vast as my canopy.

you are the rain that downpours,
and so i dance with your winds.
for my roots and leaves
save you from drowning,
as you runoff into the river.

|| rice paddies ||

scaling along the mountainsides,
rice paddies are flooded
with the monsoon's rain.
the terracing ponds are a maze,
in which we both have lost our ways.

but the harvest is here,
and it rains rice and reeds.
yet we are trapped in two different tiers.
set adrift in a labyrinth of unknown waters,
that we are unable to read.

|| mouths ||

we are just two lazy rivers
who's mouths met
and poured into one another.

|| erosion ||

like a rocky beach,
your edges were jagged and stubborn.
but like the moon
you pushed, and i pulled.
i brushed up against you
as the sea does the shore.
caressing you until there was nothing left
but raw salt.
ebbing and flowing until finally,
the water was salty.
no longer pure.

|| tides ||

every ocean has waves
that come and go.
no two tides are alike.
their rising crests eventually crash
upon the shore,
and are pulled back
into the depths of the ocean.
but the water is the same,
and will always return to the shore
who can never be too sure
of the ocean's turbulence.

|| depth ||

from the beach afar,
the ocean seems so tranquil.
calm as the waves crash,
serene as it soaks into the sand.
but enter the water,
and you will see
how tall the tides truly are,
and how deep the shallows are
even for you.

|| cyclones ||

we loved in cyclones
howling from the same winds
but never storming together.
never calm at once
and never spinning in harmony.
yet still we spun,
although on our own,
we were reckless.

we uprooted trees,
stripped them of their bark
and rid them of the branches
that were too weak to withstand.
and yet the trees thanked us,
for we had made them new.

|| tsunami ||

even water rises again after it falls.
and we are made of water,
always stirring,
hoping to rise higher than one another.
but when the crest of our waves
had touched the sun,
and we finally merged together as one,
the earth was devastated
for she was not ready to bear us.

‖ geyser ‖

stagnant at times,
the earth lies dormant.
why must she slumber,
only soon to rumble
like a geyser,
gushing forth scalding water
from the dark wombs of the earth.

|| lagoon ||

atop the volcano
lies a leaky lagoon
cradled within its crater.
so long as you are dormant,
i will try to soothe you,
before i am rolled into vapor.

|| humidity ||

there is too much water in the air
that you cannot see.
thus a dense ocean lies
upon your weighted shoulders.
i am slick as the moisture,
that effuses into your lungs
as you breathe.

|| onsen ||

the tip of the toe tells it is tepid.
and so i immerse myself in your bath,
and as the steam rises,
i too dissolve into you,
as the minerals do.

|| sauna ||

the sun is searing,
but our tears exhaust its flames.
and in this mist
our memories brew.
and in those flames,
fantasies of you,
sweat through my skin,
as i expel all of you.

|| dearly beloved ||

dear beloved,
my dearly beloved,

how harsh time passes.
yet our love remains gentle,
soft, pure, tense, and fragile.
not broken, but aged by time.
by the moments we could never share,
by the people who pried our fingers apart,
by those who marveled at our sorrows
and collected our tears by each drop,
rendering us dry. heartless beings, no longer sentient.
though time will not retrace,
our memories can.
reminisce the time when we were once divine.
divinity is unchallenged, and so remains us.

dear beloved,
my dearly beloved,

the past was decided,
and though the present seems so bleak,
let our paths knot once more.

hëat

the light and warmth
of a flame is lustful,
yet also wicked.

|| sparks ||

bright beams burst
before two lips touch and twine.
such sparks meet silence.

|| kindle ||

a little fire kindles.
like a naïve heartbeat,
embers fly and draw caution
as the wood cracks into cinders.

whether an innocent flame
or an insatiable wildfire,
every fire is doomed
to combust into ash.

|| jugni ||

we are two wandering flames
flickering among fumes
like fireflies scattering
through the night.
but we are doomed
to lay rest upon pyres,
for the sun will soon rise
and dissipate our glows.

|| wildflower ||

amidst the brambles,
hid a frail budding wildflower.
although once it finally bloomed,
a wildfire was lit.
so ferocious,
that no amount of rainfall
was able to conquer it.
only until the flames exceeded the forest,
did it fade.

|| phul ||

across the green meadow,
a fire is ablaze
as marigolds bask in the sun.
fiery hues tantalize and dance
across the horizon.

their buds riskily bloom.
exposing their petals to the nourishing,
yet heartless sunrays.

these daring flowers,
burn even brighter than the stars,
for they carry life within them.
it is their fire that i envy,
not the stars.

|| if ||

if i were a rose,
with just a slight tilt,
say you'll stay by me
and never let me wilt.

if you were the sun,
and melted me dry,
i'd be the ocean,
exposed as vast as the sky.

because if you were a fire,
fierce and untouchable
i'd be your tinder,
forever as your fuel.

if you were the winds,
sharp and violent;
and i was the trees that you had bent,
i'd stay by your side,
and endure all your torment.

yet if i was a boulder,
jagged and stubborn;
by the end of the day,
i'd be the sand that you walk on.

|| lips ||

lost in the sunset,
the horizon breathes a fire
that is soft and radiant,
like your lips stained with rouge.

if i touched them,
i would get burned
from their tender warmth.

if i kissed them,
i would smear color across the supple sky
and write our names together.

if i tasted them,
i would melt across them
like the red juice of a plum as you bite into it.
i would pool into every crevice of your plump lips,
leaving stains upon the glass you drink from.

yet if i found the sunrise
i would awaken to see
your bare face glowing
brighter than the moon.

|| bouquet ||

my heart as a prism,
i bent a rainbow
to refract its rays from the sky.
its photons scattered across the earth,
and faded within the soil.

soon after, the vivid flames bloomed
into a garden of fire.
ignited in every color of the spectrum.
its colors were radiant, fierce and lithe.

and while they danced together
to their crackling melodies,
their heat was scorching.
and so i plucked each one charily,
gathering an array of beams,
to bring to you a bouquet of flames
that flowed like a gentle heartbeat.

|| nāga ||

there is aag brewing within my lungs.
and every breath dances
to the raga set by your heartbeat.
yet if i got close enough,
to even whisper,
i would burn you.
and like a nāga,
i would be feared by all,
even if my ephemeral fire
burned blue only for you.

|| hanabi ||

as night shatters the sky,
i race through the meadow.
bamboo whispering past my ears,
sharing their secrets,
they guide me to the festival of lights.

colors and hues revealed
i wait for the sparks to fly.
the ignitions our signal,
our secret rendezvous.
the sparklers pose as our crowd,
insignificant
to the true luminescence that awaits.

as the fireworks are lit,
i watch the fragile kindles
grow into a flaming dragon.
my eyes follow as i hold its hand,
my smile brightens.
once again this year i am reunited with you.
you who fell from the stars.

but soon the beams weaken
and incinerate as they fade away
with my sobbing breaths
for yet another year of silence.

|| toxic ||

my dreams of you are simply euphoric,
your echoing voice is noxiously melodic.
i try to resist your trance,
a manipulative dance.

you radiate through my body
and permeate through my mind.
to the point that it's toxic,
i can barely survive.

your essence is simply cosmic,
you're the reason i'm alive.
you're the gin inside my tonic,
and for that numbness i strive.

diffuse from high to low,
this love is hypertonic.
absorbing my energy,
in hopes to be isotonic.

your love is volatile,
like a poisonous fire.
this dance is dangerous,
a harmonious hazard.

|| cosmic ||

my vigorous vigil
never loses its stare.
like the hands of the falling,
grasping away from despair.

this gravitational force, oh how it compels!
a magnitude even supernovas cannot repel.
your eyes surpass galaxies, each a new universe.
its stars so trivial, are all interspersed.

these constellations are the new road i travel.
your influence is devastating, a cosmic spell.
while this love is alluring,
though a malevolent curse,
its effects are eternal,
cannot see reverse.

this world you gave me appears so infinite.
afloat for æons, surpasses buoyant.
this sensation, stars cannot fathom.
lost in your clutch, a relentless chasm.

but still i try, my efforts an obscure language.
even your words, i am unworthy to salvage.
to you so small, not even an atom.
i revoke my eyes, unworthy of your phantom.

|| collide ||

even the stars pale
to the heat that radiates
from our two bodies colliding.

|| fusion ||

the sun fuses atoms together
within its core.
perhaps that is where we were born,
before we were sent to the earth,
via heat and light waves,
destined to only fuse once again.

|| lust ||

resist the temptation of lust
and trust that what you have is enough
for even the stars eventually rust,
and one day become star dust.

|| star-crossed lovers ||

the day our paths cross again
will be the day the stars fall
and the sky embraces the earth.

|| chaand raat ||

we are two halves of the same moon.
we were once full,
and they would rejoice at the sight of us.

but as each night fades,
so do we.
and so do the hands
that adorned our names.

now all we have left
is to wait.
until we are new again.
and remember that
even after the darkest of nights,
the sun will still always rise again.

|| sky ||

some skies are so dense
that its stars cannot be seen.
even if we may share the same skies
and the same stars,
it is the distance between
you and i that makes
my blank sky opaque
and your crowded sky awake.

|| aagneepath ||

i feared to walk towards you,
upon the burning coals
that you had laid out for me.
yet as it cracked,
it whispered my name,
teasing and humming:
aaja gun gun guna re.

with my bare feet
i treaded with haste
upon the path of fire.
i ran faster than i ever have to you,
never tiring or once looking back.
in sweat, tears, and blood i arrived
with everything i had,
ready to fall into your embrace.

(inspired by harivansh rai bachchan)

|| instinct ||

yes the fire is dazzling,
and its warmth so passionate,
but you have already learned long ago
that the lust of a fire is dangerous.
and yet like instinct you still touch it,
and like instinct you pull away.

|| chirbathi ||

past the darkness,
neck deep into the marshes,
i saw a dancing drop of light.
red, blue, yellow it flickered.
and so i followed.

but as my fishing boat began to sink,
the light guided me to land
towards the arid salt flats,
where the river no longer flowed.

straying distantly from my path,
it played hide and seek,
until i was lost.
though it never sought.

its presence was haunting.
intangible like a ghostly fire.
and when i touched it,
i felt nothing,
yet still i burned.
and was unable to revoke my own hand.

dragged long past the desert,
it was too late before i realized
that i had long been cursed
to follow the will-o'-the-wisp
through the weeping hollows forever.

|| touch ||

our love was the fire
that i was too nervous to touch.
yet when i burned myself,
i accepted the fault in my scars.
but when you burned me,
it was so painful,
that i screamed.

|| candle clock ||

you are the flame that melts the wax,
i am the mold that keeps it from pouring over.
but a candle can only stay lit,
so long as its wick allows it to be.
and our candle keeps sparking,
like a ticking clock
and we, my old flame,
are running out of time.

|| agarbathi ||

i rolled our essence
across sticks of bamboo
and ignited them,
to renew our lost sparks.
although it was fragrant,
the flame was faint and slow.
even the match that set it alight burned brighter.

yet i yearned for us to keep burning.
but our fragrance was dimming
and our stick had fallen to brittle ashes,
which you blew away without hesitation.
hastily i tried to breathe life back into our flame,
but it was senseless.
for our flame was already but a mere orange glow.

i cupped the fragile flame within my hands
as it dwindled away.
but against my efforts,
you suffocated it with your fingertips.
leaving our hands covered in singes.
and just like incense
we burned out of lust,
as our scent faded into evanescence.

|| petal ||

a flower blooms forth from the sullen earth,
each petal reaching forward towards the sun.
its rays unattainable and harsh,
yet sustaining of life.

as the petals stretch further in infatuation,
water unable to provide turgidity,
each petal falls,
lifeless and alone in the soil.

|| darjeeling ||

i handpicked you among gardens.
our memories were so abundant,
that i carried basketfuls upon my back,
across the peaks and valleys
of the green darjeeling hills.

i sundried you gingerly.
yet within a blink of an eye,
you ignited into flames and ran ablaze.
hanging gardens fell into cinders,
as soft soot rose to the sky,
and burned my eyes.
your smoke was an echo
of the flavor that never became.

and as i tried to save your essence,
tears fell into the teacup that i held for you.
but even your blackened brew was insipid.
leaving the most bitter aftertaste,
to the sharpest of tongues.

if only i had tasted you sooner,
for our tongues only sense bitterness
to warn us of poisons.
but your aroma was a ruse,
that i never thought to diffuse.

|| lava ||

i moved mountains for you
yet still you wanted more.
for the snowcapped mountains,
were too frigid for your desires.

and so from the earth,
i erupted volcanos to melt the snow.
but it was futile.
for the lava was volatile,
more fluid than water,
and deteriorated everything within its flow.
even you,
who was smothering within the ashes.

in sorrow i parted the seas for you.
the smoke burning our lungs,
i extended my hand
to offer you solace
before the lava could carry you away.
but you were mired,
intoxicated by the dense smoke.
sintered in soot,
you spurned my hand.

finally, you opened your stone eyes
only to see the grim river flowing before you.
but you were already petrified in anguish.
and the lava inevitably came,
to sweep the statue of you away,
as you molted into the raging river.

|| fission ||

under intense pressure
an atom splits even further.
– imagine splitting two parts of a whole,
that never sought to be separated.
the pain is wrenching.
and when it screams,
it is known to the world.

|| darwaza ||

you drilled towards the earth's core
to dig my own grave.
but instead unleashed the gates of hell,
where an ephemeral fire was set to the pyre,
calling your name.

i grasped your hand to save you,
but you clawed your nails into my palms.
and as you struggled to pull me in with you,
you slipped from my fingertips,
crashing away into your own flames
ready to return home.

|| jahannam ||

remain as you are
for there is hope no longer,
even jahannam lies at your feet
and trembles to hold you.

boil

when left unkempt
love continues to roll,
until it boils over.

|| thorn ||

you were a thorn among roses
and pricked me every time
i drew closer.

|| honey ||

there are other bees
who want to make toxic honey
from your sweet nectar.

|| moth ||

i am a moth who seeks
but is never sought.
i long to be like the butterflies
whom you chase after
and let drink nectar
from your gardens.

|| queen bee ||

i was like a drone,
caught for only a moment in flight.
then you moved on
to start your own colony
as i fell to the earth
paralyzed.

|| pairs ||

and we created you in pairs,
but perhaps i was not...

|| wicked ||

you were the fog
that obstructed my vision.
that loomed into a dense nimbus,
warning me of what was brewing.
yet still i walked blindly
into the funnel
of your wicked tornado.

|| patang ||

you light the sky,
like thousands of kites on festival day.
children race one another,
losing their breath as they laugh and tumble.
sweating as the blazing sun
makes rhythms upon their backs.
colors adorn their scarves and ornate clothing
as they parade to watch you fly.
every kite a unique design,
so fragile and gentle
yet sturdy and tall.
stretching higher and further
as everyone marvels at their glory below.

but you command the sky.
your beauty and proximity
to the heavens is unmatched.

i am the string that keeps you grounded,
saving you from straying too far away from home,
yet you said i was holding you back.

however, there are other strings in the sky:
sharper and longer.
and they chase after you,
and now have grown dangerously close.

i tried to tug you closer to me,
yet you said i was holding you back.
so you reached even further away
until our string was taught
– and with a single sudden touch,
our connection was snipped.
and you plummeted towards the earth,
hoping another string would catch you.
but my frayed ends were unable to make new ties,
and i too drifted away into the distance.

|| man ||

move the moons,
split the seas,
wield the winds,
and touch the stars.
what i would, if i could,
but i am just a man,
weaker than wood,
marred by wounds and scars.

|| mausam ||

you said forever and always
and you held my hand for years.
our intimacy was unmatched,
and i knew we would never part.
but then one day the weather changed,
and you were no longer near.

you were just a season
that comes and goes
and now i am just a person
that you no longer know.

|| cliffhanger ||

the soonest i stepped forward,
you took one step back.
slowly edging on to
the precipice of your fingertips
as you took your sweet time.
and yet somehow,
i was the one to fall
in love with the barren earth,
because that is where you saw my worth.

|| crowded chaatri ||

like your shadow,
i have never left your side.
for as many years as we have strolled
along this stone path,
i have silently listened to your every breath,
and every heartbeat.
i matched your rhythms with:
the heavy rain that ended each summer,
the crunching sounds as fallen leaves were stepped on,
the early snow that warned us of winter,
and the sailing of blossoms as each spring passed us by.
i was the wind in the seasons that we shared,
who helped you land gracefully to the earth.

but today in this storm,
i struggle to keep our umbrella high.
enough to keep you dry.
so much that my shoulder drips,
but i hide the pain from my aching arm
behind my smile that you no longer notice.

yet now our umbrella has become crowded,
though i no longer stand beneath.
but remember,
there was no one who has loved you more,
enough to realize,
that the sun has never stopped shining
through this storm whose eye was you.
that the seasons only change,
because the axis of earth is you,
and my entire world revolves solely around you.

|| khajoor ||

i broke the winds for you
as sharp sand storms
pierced my skin.
i longed to give you shade,
as the sun charred my back.
you asked to be fed,
i gave you acaís.
i sent coconuts across the ocean
to quench your thirst.
how grueling it was
to bear dates for you
from the sand,
yet still i was not enough.
for you cut me open
to rip my hearts out
longing to make wine
from my sap.

|| anar ||

you overflowed my heart,
until it was swollen past full bloom.
you split it open to find
thousands of arils
spilling forth from its honeycomb.
you ripped it apart chamber by chamber,
as red juices bled out from its atriums
and pooled down into your palms.
you beat it dry,
gutting the fruits of life to taste,
until it was nothing
but an empty shell.

|| hourglass ||

i carved my soul out from my very core,
and poured it into your cupped hands.
spilling like a ticking hourglass.
each grain of sand a precious story,
a memory that has journeyed across worlds.
but you were impatient,
you asked for more where there was none,
and shattered the glass to gut it of sand and salt.
you poured that very sand into a doll
and poked it with pins and needles,
turning it into a writhing cactus.
you held the earth within your very hands,
and had the chance to nurture a garden,
yet you deprived it of life,
leaving it a barren desert.

|| saans ||

every breath you take,
you take him with you.
as you exhale,
he brushes along your tongue.
he knows your words
before they leave your lips.
each breath fortifies you of life,
expands your lungs
and rushes to your heart.
he keeps you beating,
roams you freely,
where i cannot.
he is there where i should be,
where i want to be.

he taunts me when you laugh,
and when you breathe deeply.
he is the air in my despair.

|| lunar eclipse ||

we had always faced one another,
never once looking back.
until you found the sun
whose gravity was stronger,
and we fell into syzygy
where i was left alone
in your shadow
to form a dark side.

|| the dark side of the moon ||

you are like the moon
who's beauty glows
and emanates the world,
yet two faced
with a dark side
that makes even
the sun and stars
weep and whirl.

|| moor ||

perched atop the canopies,
flaunting my crest like a crown
i called for your name.
yet you hissed in reply
and ruffled my feathers.

but still you were hypnotizing.
whispering to fan out my train:
royal blue, emerald green and auspicious gold
all eyes were on me,
except your snake eyes.

still i yearned to mesmerize you.
with my exquisite beauty,
daring dances and sultry songs.
but your black skin was thick
and you paid no attention to me.
instead you shamed me
for my bare black legs,
the same legs you gave me.

and as i wept in flight,
twisting and tangling,
you sunk your fangs into my talons,
paralyzing me
as i crashed into the earth.

|| sapera ||

it is futile to charm a cobra,
for she herself is deaf
and can never be hypnotized.
she is unable to hear
the eloquent melodies
of the pungi you play.

but you can.
and you will be charmed
into believing that you have earned her trust.
but she will always see you as a threat,
and when you are most vulnerable,
she will strike and leave you bitten
before she molts her skin
to find her next victim.

|| acid rain ||

i was the earth aching for the rain.
not knowing that you had
mixed and mingled with other gasses
becoming corrosive to the touch.

|| scald ||

i never learned
that steam burns hotter
than boiling water
until i touched you.

|| jala ||

you never knew how to make
the simplest cup of chai.
you were much too impatient
to wait until it rolled,
always walking away in confidence.

but when you leave it unattended,
you anger it.
and it boils over, uncontained.
burning across the pot and stove,
until it helplessly weeps
as you hastily return to scrape it to nothing.

|| rusk ||

i was the rusk you dunked into your chai.
that you were too excited to taste.
that you soaked me with more tea
than i could hold.
until i broke apart and dissolved
as you tried fishing me out
with another piece of rusk.

|| qurbaan ||

my heart, my soul
was all i had
and both i sacrifice to you.
i have nothing left
to my name but yours.
only yours.

my entire being aches
to become one with you,
but i fear that only one
can never be enough for you.

|| fitoor ||

with you i am helpless.
my every thought
becomes of you
and still it is you
who i cannot understand.
am i madly in love
or mad to still love you?

i am no longer my own,
for you have consumed me.
and yet that is what i love most
about myself.
you.

|| thawed |||

maybe i'm still drawn to you
because i'm so frigid and alone inside.
maybe your warmth is all i know,
and i was just ready to be thawed.
or maybe i'd just rather scream
and be boiled alive.

|| raja ||

sitting upon my gold throne
i gaze upon my kingdom.
my head weighed down by the taaj i carry,
i weigh if i truly have the wisdom
to carry this kingdom upon my shoulders.

my head bowed down by the weight i carry,
i beg to be freed of this burden.
listening to the songs of the canary
before it passes,
i too pass my kingdom
for a life in luxury,
freed from your rule.

|| to the man that loves her next ||

to the man that loves her next
love her to the distance that i came short of.
love her past the moon and back
because meeting her halfway wasn't enough.
love her from the sky to the sea,
because she wants you to fall harder
from the pedestal she placed you upon
and down to earth.
love her deeper than the depths of the sea.
leagues into her beating heart,
until you drown, gasping for air,
suffocating into darkness.
she will be the breath of air
that is so fortifying of life.
the cold air that slides past your tongue
and swells into your lungs,
she will be inside you.
she will be the ray of light that shatters silence
and splits the darkness into millions of fragments.
fragments that she will sharpen
and use to carve her way into your mind.
she will consume every thought
your brain can fathom.
she will be the light to your lens,
whether they are open or shut.
her face will never escape you.
an image so pristine, yet intangible.
she is a mirage.

to the man that loves her next
she will become your entity.

but to the man that loves her next
one miscalculated moment,
a single strident word,
an unspoken gesture,
will be your demise.
an entity you once revered a goddess from heaven,
will become a demon from hell.
she will throw your world asunder,
every sound will transpose as thunder,
every vision will blister your eyes,
every memory an excruciating torment,
every breath insufficient, unable to sustain life.
and you will wither like a writhing flower
reabsorbed into the dirt that she walks on,
as if you were nothing.

to the fool that loves her next
don't.

where love hides,
hate seeks and finds a home.

|| half & half ||

imagine never feeling comfortable
in your own skin.
to live your life as only half of who you are
because you do not possess
the words to express the other half.
and so your soul remains lost in translation,
because this was never the language
you used to define yourself.

|| barfi ||

how can you be so color blind
when even the snow can scatter
in colors and flavors.
condensed milk mixed with
coconuts, cardomoms, and pistachios
crowned with silver leaves of vark.
we are a spectrum of colors,
everything nature has to offer
is in us too.
we are an entire delicacy
and yet you remain decadent.

|| half a cup of chai ||

every morning when i would wake up
there would be half a cup of chai left on the stove.
my mother would already be at work by now,
working until her bones ached.
and although my siblings hated chai,
my mother made sure
that her last child was addicted at a young age.
but there it was, my favorite part of the day,
sitting upon the stove.
the reminder that my mother remembered.
i know now that she wanted to be there with me,
but she couldn't.
she wanted to sit down with me,
chatting away while dunking cake rusk into our chai
until it would break off,
just like she did on the weekends.
but to a five-year-old,
i was just happy to have this cup of chai.
well half a cup,
because my mother said i was too young.
and even though the chai tasted off
after sitting around and being microwaved again,
i still drank every last drop because i was so grateful.

as i grew older,
my mother would always make me the chaiwala
whenever guests would come over.
i hated it.
but it gave me years of practice to master the perfect
recipe for doodh pathi,
even if it was different from my mother's own recipe:
i liked masala, she liked peekha.

now whenever i brew a pot of chai for myself,
i think about setting out another mug
as my mother had done for me.
but instead, i silently sip
and savor those memories of the lonely days
that we could never spend together.
like i did as a child.

|| fall ||

our skin is the color of fall,
the season in which you flourish in,
and yet still you go out of your way
to walk all over and step on us
as if we are just crisp and fallen leaves.

|| rude ||

i longed to be a part of you
because you look like me
or rather you took from me
while never once looking at me.

— *minorities*

|| homeless ||

i rejected the culture
that i was conceived from
and still was not accepted
into the one that i was born into.
i am homeless,
yet i chose to be.

|| unwanted ||

i am like a moth that seeks
light and nectar through the darkness,
just as the butterflies do.
i am so close to being the same,
yet not enough to be wanted.

|| a forgotten people ||

sitting next to my desk lamp,
i stare at a blank page that is blinding white
like the flashing gunshots of rifles.
my mind enters chaos
like the cannons ricocheting against our fortresses.
my hand quivers to reach
for my choice of wielded weapon:
pen or pencil.
i traumatically hesitate to click the pen,
as it taunts me like the cocking of rifles.
the mechanical pen juxtaposes
against the traditional wooden pencil:

the ink flowing through the pen to paper
is a reminder of the blood spilled by my people
defending our borders.
just like any paper, once written on,
the marks cannot be erased.
yet this bloodshed leaves a permanent mark
on an erasable culture,
a dark spot in history that will soon be forgotten
as more pages are marked on.

the pencil eraser is a reminder of a culture
doomed to be forgotten.
as the eraser shreds left by abrasion
are the fragments of a forgotten people.
the pencil tip that becomes weaker
the more it is worn down,
never stood a chance.

suddenly, the pencil tip snaps.
and the lead dust scattered across the desk
is a diaspora of people,
lost and dismembered.
what was once an astute pencil tip
is now a blunt edge,
unable to leave a mark on a page.

|| salt ||

salt dissolves completely in water.
i yearn to find that level of belonging.
how long must i wait
until others finally realize
that salt can never be separated from water
with just their bare hands alone.

(inspired by nayyirah waheed)

|| palates of memories ||

the first time i made masala chai
was with my father.
my mother had asked me to make her chai
to soothe yet another throbbing headache.

and so my father showed me
what spices were fit for tea.
i watched as he dropped cloves, cinnamon,
and cardamoms into the pot.
in excitement i threw in ginger, turmeric, fennel,
star anise, black pepper and everything else.

we were proud of the outcome
but when she finally took a sip,
she made a hesitant face when the spices hit her.
when i implored, she said
"every now and then,
masala chai is nice to have."

what is exotic to some, is common to others.
not all people need flavors to remind them of home
because they may taste them elsewhere.
or rather, everyone has different palates of memories.

|| lucky ||

the scar that runs
along my mother's belly
is a reminder that i am
lucky.

|| wisteria ||

parents always support us.
they bear our weight,
even when they cannot bear their own.
they ache to see us blossom
and shower the sky in purples and violets,
knowing full well that they never could.

we only hang tall,
because grounded to the earth
are roots that desperately gather water
to quench the thirsts of the sky.
and *maybe* there are times,
when the fragrance of the wisteria
reaches the earth.
but rarely does the inflorescence
ever look down to see
the havoc that our vines have wreaked.
that we are strangling,
the very trunks and roots that support us.

|| mother's tongue ||

the unspoken words
that hide behind her tongue,
are like the hundreds of lullabies
that she had sung
as you were screaming
when you were so young.

yet still you say the harsh words
that leave your sharp tongue.
and so she bites her own as she sobs
knowing how much wisdom she has to share
in her mother tongue.

|| calloused hands ||

the tears and love of my mother
are tattooed across her hands and arms
in the forms of burns and scars.
to keep moving
at the expense of her own body
and her own happiness
only she can do.
these burdened hands
that even my own rough hands
are forever unworthy to hold,
because the weights that inflicted them
are as different as a lump of coal
and a heart of gold.
because in her eyes
it was never a burden at all.

|| chambeli ||

i knew spring was drawing near
when i would ride my bike home from school
and smell the unripen fragrance of budding jasmines
along my path.

– my mother had told me
how her old home in pakistan
was covered in vines and shrubs of jasmines.
and how her grandfather would make
garlands for her grandmother
every morning before she woke up.

and so once they finally blossomed,
i would rush to the park
and gather as many jasmines as i could call mine.
i would steal some string from the royal dansk tin
and struggle to pass it through the needle
to make as many garlands for my mother as i could
before she came home.
one for her wrist, one for her neck,
and one for her ankle.

i wanted to help her remember her homeland,
as if she could have ever forgotten.
and with a smile on her face,
she would wear them all day
until they finally shriveled and fell apart.

|| daughters ||

daughters are like a budding flower.
they are so precious,
and have so much potential for greatness.
but if you do not give her water
and let her see the sun,
then her roots can never grow
bigger than the pot that contains her.
and she will stay drooping
as each season passes her by,
while she dreams for the spring
when she can spread her roots
and finally blossom.

|| taj mahal ||

a woman's body is her temple
a sacred palace of worship.
and a man's job is but to stand watch
outside her temple,
as she continues to stand tall.

he must never restrain
abuse
defile
or define her respect
for she defines her own.

|| a business deal ||

my father sat me down once to listen
as he told my sister that
marriage is a business deal,
like an exchange of goods,
and i had never seen her so
broken.

|| shehr ||

sons are raised as tigers.
like innocent cubs
that never leave their mother's side.
they are loved and nurtured blindly,
always pouncing upon one another,
as they secretly hone their hunting skills.

until finally they outgrow family
and run away to live in solitude,
never to return home.
ferocious and shameless
they ambush prey after prey,
heralding wars on end.
mating upon whims,
they foster their kin
to do the same.
to follow their instints
and never once feel remorse.

|| sex ||

it's a clever strategy to taboo sex
and then force it upon women
so that they cannot voice their grief.

but tabooing sex is not the solution
rather it provides the perfect alibi.
instead, hold a man accountable
for his inhumanity for once.

if he forces himself upon you
to assert his already fragile dominance,
that does not make him any more of a man.
rather, it makes him pathetic,
and desperate for the serendipity
that he is not man enough
to earn respectfully.

|| haathiyon ||

like elephants
we remember everything,
our tusks that were cut for ivory.
our hides skinned for leather.
how can you hunt us for our beauty
yet leave us naked in the safari.
accusing us of musth
when we defend ourselves.

we remember everything.
but now our herd will be heard.
painting our skin in mandalas,
adorning our heads in crowns,
the very dirt upon our skin
will become clouds of rang
as we stampede to reclaim our throne.
you trained us for battle,
and we will be triumphant.

|| bhai jaan ||

when we were young
my brother and i shared a bed.
seven years apart in age,
yet we have always been so close.
we shared many conversations in the dark.
and every single night,
before he would fall asleep,
he would roll over to his side
and without fail,
never forget to say
"just because i'm not facing you,
doesn't mean i don't love you."

and thats how i know,
no matter the distance,
nothing will ever change.

|| tattoos ||

if the flowers that adorn my hands
make me any less of a man,
then i will paint gardens
and wear my heart upon my sleeve,
and show you just how
elegant a man can be.

|| approval ||

wether or not
you approve of me,
is not of my concern.
aunty ji.

|| lingua franca ||

patiently waiting
for your chance to interject
is not the same as listening.

you forbade my voice,
thus to you i never spoke.
now you are alone.

— *the gap between generations*

|| lowest of lows ||

respect is not deserved,
nor is it served to those undeserving.
but rather it is earned by those
who have served the givers
who in turn the givers they respect.

but to assume you have respect,
to beg and demand to be given
is the lowest of lows
that warrants disrespect.

– demanding elders

|| blood ||

i shiver at the touch
of my own blood
because of how foreign
and longing
it has become.

|| unwritten ||

i only wrote about what i knew
thus i never wrote about you.

the words i could not say to you
or rather you would not listen to
i wrote here.

– *elders know best*

|| aam ||

during mango season,
my father would always ask me
to pick out the ripest mango
for him to peel and cut for me.
he would hold out his hand
like an offering of love,
sacrificing a slice of his favorite fruit.
wanting to share the memories
of his own childhood with me
as his father had shared
over mangos with him.

and as the juices dripped
down his hands of promise,
i rejected his countless offers
every single time out of resentment.
even though the lump in my throat
also yearned for my favorite fruit…

i am sorry,
baba jaan.

|| geometry ||

not all minds will parallel with mine.
in fact, many will intersect.
yet if you parallel with me,
i will connect the dots to you.
but my vision is unwavering
and i will walk my straightest line.

strain

when love becomes straining,
let it drain.

|| bleed ||

i will bloom so loudly
that your ears will bleed.

|| wet wood ||

loving you was like
trying to ignite a fire
to wet wood.

|| tangled ||

you left me like an unkempt garden
whose thorns, thistles, and tendrils
were all in tangles.
i strained to unravel myself.
until i finally accepted
what could never be untied
and decided to bloom forward.
leaving my roots and soil impenetrable
from ever being uprooted again.

|| anjeer ||

thousands of flowers flourish in secrecy,
yet unfolding those secrets is futile.
do not be fooled,
for although the fig is without a pit,
inside lies a wasp in its place.
beauty is found where it cannot be seen
yet so is pity.

|| love at first sight ||

if love at first sight truly existed,
then you must not have seen me,
for you would have never resisted.

|| cupid's arrow ||

a shooting star falls
and pierces my aching heart.
and as i bleed a river of sorrows
that guides me past you

i look down
to see my own reflection.

|| rafflesia ||

bearing no roots of its own,
feeding off others,
the bud of the rafflesia
connives for months.
until at night it finally blooms.
only to be covered in warts
and wreak of rotting flesh.
it repulses beauty itself,
and is doomed to decay days later.
it seldom blossoms
as only flies are attracted
to the rancid nectar
of the rafflesia.

|| mautam ||

even the grasses we tread upon,
can tower above our heads
before we have the chance to turn them.

yet there are times when a century passes us by
within a moment.
and that is when the bamboo finally blooms.
but only when the bamboo blossoms
is it a premonition of impending doom.
for its flowers weep across the canopy,
shedding rice like a storm of tears,
black rats scurry in mischief
to reap the fruits of our famines;
passing their maladies upon us.
and soon the sole bamboo shoot,
that carried the entire forest upon its shoulders,
falls.

not every flower is fated
to be the harbingers of life
as we expect of them.

|| wither ||

gardens blossomed upon our steps.
yet the more i walked aloned,
the more the gardens grew.
i realize now that
i'd rather blossom alone,
than wither away with you.

|| welwitschia ||

for a thousand years
i withstood the barren earth
and i will again for a thousand years more.
because standing alone
is always better than standing you.

|| sand ||

i once poured my entire soul
into the palms of your hands
until i was empty inside.
but like sand,
you let me slip through the cracks
between your fingers,
out of fear of soiling them.

it is not your fault however,
for your hands were just simply
not designed to hold me.

|| pride ||

holding my chin high,
i stare straight into its eyes.
i swallow my pride,
not my prey
and therefore i am prouder.
i become big,
not a deception.

|| mind reader ||

the only book
i could never read
was your mind
because it had no spine.

even between the lines
i could not read
because you were too blind
to write on the lines
i drew for you.

|| wine tasting ||

let me be the wine that you drink
and savor by the drop,
so that i can be the wine that you heave
and regret you ever tasted.

|| pandora's box ||

thinking of you again
is like opening pandora's box:
all of my malevolent memories of you
overflow my world
and i am left with nothing but
hope
that i never see you again.

|| restless ||

make him toss and turn at night
staring at the ceiling fan spin,
as his mind circles around you
over and over again.
make him restless
like you were once for him.

|| the sailing bottle ||

i once stood by the shore and bottled up my emotions,
parting ways, i sent them across the ocean.
though water seeped through, and so denser it became
i yearned that someone would write in return
the recipe to cure a sunken heart.

yet the harsh riptides were unforgiving,
and the bottle shattered amidst the sea.
dispersed across the distant shore as young sea glass.
still i yearned for the day
that someone would solve this puzzle,
and set sail a courier
with the remedy for a brackish heart.

still i stood by the shore,
alas, amidst the mist, and amidst the sea
arrived an empty bottle returned to me.
from the ocean, 'twas a potion
made of my very own emotions.

|| kohinoor ||

diamonds are born
under immense pressure.
and i was but a lump of coal,
full of imperfections.
longing to even glint
amidst the darkness.
yet every diamond is born in the rough,
and every scratch and burn
forced upon me was nothing
but buff and shine
upon my every facet.
now i am the gem that endures all.
i am the gem that entices all.
for i no longer shed blood,
but rather blood is shed for me.

|| afterthought ||

you and i are of one thinking.
it's a shame
that i was only an after thought.

|| perfect ||

any version of me
with any number of flaws
is more perfect
than any version of you
that points them out.

‖ sea salt ‖

imagine how much salt
lies unstirred at the bottom of the sea.
that must have been
where you were born.

|| noor ||

even just a drop of my noor
could absorb all of your darkness,
but i am not going to spare you.
again.

|| mourning monsoon ||

everyone yearns for your return.
because with you deserts turn green
shriveled creeks finally flow
and into the cities they follow.

but as your shadow grows soon,
as the winds begin to croon,
and as the ocean lurks closer
tugged by the moon,
you returned weeping
with more tears overflowing
than a mourning monsoon.

you wept through the night
and flooded our rivers
until finally in the morning
everyone yearned for your departure.

|| drop ||

i do not need an entire ocean to drown you,
but a drop to the tongue is enough,
for i am the entire ocean within a drop.

(inspired by rūmī)

|| soar ||

when you swiftly soared off
to find newer heights,
higher than our nest,
i finally had room
to spread my aching wings
and fly twice as high.

|| hawa ||

i will no longer let
the flow of the wind
leave me winded.
but rather it will find its flow
through my hair
while i keep pushing forward.
as i am now the force
who the wind itself fears.
for the wind is but a whisper of dust,
carried by the gales
of my own fearsome typhoon.

|| orbit ||

i was a fool to believe that
my world even once revolved around you,
when it was always my world to claim.
you were nothing but a mere moon,
lost within my orbit.

|| solar eclipse ||

how ill-fated were we
to have seen the sun silenced
under the new moon's shadow
and turn the world black.

|| kala mirch ||

across every region
and every recipe,
there is one common spice
that induces remorse
as its juices drip to the tongue.

you are the elaichi
that everyone dreads
to find in their biryani.

i am the saffron.

|| fiber ||

i realized how right you were
when you said
that i was not good enough.
we are far from equality,
for i am much greater than you.
even just an ounce of me,
would dissolve the very fiber of your being.

|| suraj ||

flowers always grow
and face towards the sun,
yet it is my radiance
that turns the heads of gardens
as i simply wander by.

|| gravity ||

for so long i felt as if shooting stars
were falling upon the earth
just to break my heart into pieces.
not realizing,
that it was simply just my gravity
ripping the very stars
straight out of the skies.

|| surahi ||

as the rain relentlessly pours down upon the rooftops,
i watch as it slowly drips into the clay earthen pots.
the drip drop sound is taunting,
and so i test the rain's temperature
with the tips of my fingers.
it is cooling.

i stick my parched tongue out
to taste the very freedom that is so soothing.
stepping into unknown territory,
i let the rain pour down upon my bare shoulders
so that the rain water absorbs into my skin
leaving behind the raw salt.
i cup the frigid water from the surahi into my palms,
rinsing myself as the salt exfoliates a new layer
from my tired skin.
it is refreshing,
and at last i am new.

|| strain ||

i have brewing inside me
the spices of darkness:
love, hate, anger, resentment.
like a rolling pot of tea it grows darker
as it saps the essence of its loose leaves
and screams to be subdued.
but at last, it is finally time
that i strain myself of all the impurities
that taint my sanctity,
and leave myself bathed
in the purest form of tea.

Savör

*life is of many flavors,
taste them.*

|| serotiny ||

there are seeds that germinate
only after a wildfire razes.
you are of those seeds.
and from it a forest will rise
from the searing earth.

|| dandelions ||

dandelions bloom in secrecy
yet writher in beauty
as they scatter through the wind.
you shall too.

|| summer storms ||

only the summer showers
can weep in heavy storms
while sunshine floods the sky in lush gold.
even the sky sheds tears of joy too.

|| thunder ||

lightning takes the path of least resistance,
yet it is the thunder who rumbles and roars,
and makes hearts sink to the earth in shock.

|| mother earth ||

if you take the path of least resistance
you will never learn to walk the earth.
to be safe, you face the dearth
of never knowing what awaits you.

until you take the road less travelled,
you will never learn her worth,
or that of which she has given to you
and what to you she has birth.

|| bird of paradise ||

there will be men
who will pluck your petals
and it will be painful.
but in time you will heal
to become the venus flytrap
that devours their thirsts
like a bird of prey,
and blossom fiercer
than a bird of paradise.

|| beauty ||

beauty is pain
only because we paint it to be.

stop searching for beauty
in other people's eyes
and start finding beauty
with your own,

*beauty is in
the eyes of the beholder.*

|| yoga ||

we twist and turn
to fit into the molds
that society has laid out for us.
we become shapes that our bodies
were never meant to be.
not realizing that
beauty comes in many forms,
and you are one of them.

|| canvas ||

those that have not shed blood
believe they are strong and unstained.
not realizing,
that it is those that have bled,
who have learned how not to bleed again.

|| nectarine ||

sometimes alongside a peach
a nectarine is born.

and while their skin feels different,
on the inside,
they taste almost the same.

and that is *okay*.

|| bloom ||

a flower cannot choose the place from where it
blooms,
nor does it compete with the flower next to it,
it just blooms.
a flower does not choose its time to blossom
nor does it choose its time to fall
but the flower that blooms in adversity
is the most rare and beautiful of all.

(inspired by: hiro mashima, zen shin, walt disney)

|| fragrance ||

a flower spills its fragrance
to even the hands
that pluck its petals.
but it is those flowers
who have the strongest fragrance,
that are handpicked among gardens.

(inspired by ali ibn abu talib)

|| tears ||

your tears are rich like honey,
more precious than liquid gold.
and like sap they are thick and heavy,
as they seal the cracks of broken hearts.

and as they ooze down
upon your barked skin,
chiming like bells,
theives gather around to
find your treasures.

but these termites you mistake for bees
saw away at the trees of life,
and tap into your fountains of fortunes,
until you run dry.

you must shed tears for no one.

|| nectar ||

only few bees can taste
the sweetness of pure nectar.
search for those tongues.

|| transparency ||

a drop of water is clear,
and yet every color within.
it reflects the colors,
it chooses to be.
and when to be.

only show your true colors,
to the eyes most worthy.
for others will only try to fade them.

|| koi ||

if the koi can survive the winter,
months beneath the frozen surface,
as frigid water draws into their gills,
so can you.

|| rinse ||

raw rice bears from the earth
yet still it is not pure.
but if you rinse and wash it,
away from its sins,
the water is bound to get clearer.

|| lotus ||

fear not,
for even within the thick mud,
a sole lotus can bloom.
even seeds sowed in shadows
can bloom forth a thousand radiant petals,
that are unstained and light the darkness.
it too will find solace,
until the sun rises again.

|| whitewater ||

you cannot change the course of the river
once it has decided its path.
even past the edge,
it will still flow.

it never hesitates to lead,
yet it is the earth that holds the river,
and even when its rapids spill over the bank,
the earth endures it.

and while it appears rousing,
it is unstable.
and its frothy white water,
although airy, is suffocating.

do not enter waters
that you know are treacherous.
just let it flow.

|| burns ||

salt burns the throat,
but its water is vital.
a flame burns to the touch,
but its heat is survival.
smoke burns the eyes,
but the air is essential.

that which burns,
can also heal,
and is not always fatal.
scars are only proof,
that you have finally healed.

|| dhyāna ||

focus.
like the blue flames
at the heart of a beating fire,
it is not stirred by the red wings
that flutter amidst the open air around it.
it just glows.

|| pankha ||

you must be the paper fan
that breathes fuel into
the river of flames inside you.
no one else.

every stroke to be a fearsome gale
as you run wild into an inferno
that is both terrifying and tranquil.

*for others will only try to smother
your budding flames.*

|| kismat ||

life is always moving,
time is always flowing,
but what is yours
shall never pass you.

|| karma ||

karma chases us like butterflies.
where it follows,
gardens blossom.
of weeds or flowers,
that is of your will.

|| hanami ||

you shower the sky in sailing blossoms
as everyone gazes upon your beauty.
yet to them from afar
as they sip from their shallow cups of saké
cherry, plum, peach, or almond
they all appear the same.

but today i have come to the festival
for my own sake.
for another excuse
to gaze upon not the sky nor its stars,
but its secrets:

your beauty is soft and gentle like sakura,
painting the sky in a pink flush
with a feathered paintbrush.
yet sharp and supple like ume,
sprinkling upon hills in snowy white
with a feathered duster.

although there are times
when your branches droop and weep,
as your flesh becomes silent and sylvan
like an almond in instar.
reminding the earth of autumn
like a feathered pillow,
as piling leaves cushion the falls of ripened fruit.

there will be a day,
when you will rise again
like a flaming apricot blossom,
piercing the sky in a sunny yellow
like a feathered arrow,
embracing the sun who once gave you life.

|| sui dhaaga ||

a kite struggles to find lift,
yet it finds comfort within the earth.
roaming through rivers,
drifting through spirits,
lost with no destination.

yet weaving between stars,
and twisting through rivers,
a string unearths a kite.
like thread piercing a needle,
it takes flight,
with its destiny burning
just past the longing horizon.

|| ghumeya ||

as the sun falls
i travel where the path takes me
searching for nothing defined.
wandering through countless bazaars
listening to the dhols and tablas of the night
and drifting through the diya stricken rivers.
my feet cannot stay still
nor my heart it keeps searching.
even settling down for slumber drives it restless
as my ears wander through the busy streets,
searching –
for the salt and sugar that taste the same
the sand and sea that feel the same
the sun and shade that are devoid.

it is time to return home
the only haven
my wandering heart has ever known.

|| holi ||

a fire burns deeply,
turning its offerings to ash.
ash that burns into colors.

as spring scurries across the earth
and scatters in patterns of rangoli,
nature blossoms the ingredients for holi.

the mehndi and haldi
that become a vivid green and yellow,
the dyes of tesu, alma, and indigo
await you.

rang dances across the sky.
staining your skin,
healing your skin,
as you embrace the hues of birth,
you glow.

all eyes lay upon your colored skin,
like a sindoor running across your forehead.
you have seen the depths of life.
running through your veins,
among a canvas of white,
you bleed in rich color.

for it is when they stare,
that they envy the knowing of life in color.

|| parwana ||

not all love is as seamless
as chrysalis to crowns.
every heart undergoes metamorphosis,
having wounds that have been stitched back together.
it is not seamless.
and although it is easier,
to hide yourself within a cocoon and sit still,
there is beauty hidden within you.
hibernating, as you heal upon your own pace.

but even that very same cocoon
can be unraveled and woven
to create a love that is softer than silk.
and from it will emerge a sheer moth,
that will be sought after.
even more so than monarchs and emperors.
for its ability to always find the light
within the nighttime darkness
is unparalleled.
while butterflies were given crowns at birth,
moths have earned their royalty.

|| sitara ||

the stars did not choose to shine at night
because they longed to be seen.
for the stars are always burning.
but it is the sky who yearned
to see the stars shine
and silenced itself.

i want to burn as the stars do,
not worrying about who sees
or what they think.
unstirred by the whims of those around it.

|| galaxy ||

i want to pull you into my arms
like the sun pulls planets into its orbit.
keeping you warm,
until the beating flames within me
cease to burn any longer.

|| kainaat ||

your mind is as expansive
as the universe.
and still even that does not
do it justice.

|| taqat ||

the force of us coming together
is the sound of an entire universe
bursting into existence.

|| spilled chai ||

so many memories i have shared with you
over just a cup of chai.
i long to share many more with you.

how do you take it jaan?
how much sugar, how much milk.
tell me so that i can perfect
your recipe.

my love, my secrets, my soul
how much do you need?
because i cannot stop pouring.
the cup is past full,
spilling over the edges
and yet i am not empty.

how is it that you hold so much of me
and never tire.
how is it that you trust so much
in our belonging.

tell me jaan.
how can it be
that *our* recipe
is so. damn. perfect.

alyees qureshi

|| pairs ||

and we created you in pairs
but perhaps i was not.
or rather,
we had always been
created as one.

|| zyka ||

growing up, i tried to veil my heritage
with as much body spray it took to hide
the smell of spices in my clothing,
in my hair, in my skin.
so that no one would notice that i didn't fit in,
or rather smell that i was different.

i would come home as my mother was cooking
and scurry to my room
before the oil in the air could sink in.
slamming the door shut
and racing for the lavender air freshener,
to sit in a cloud until dinner was ready.
and still i ate in my room to avoid not the spices
but the conversation.

but once i finally left home
i missed not the meals but the spices:
the flavors that added authenticity to my falsified life.
the dishes that my mom prepared so often
that i thought would be better without this or that
were not so easy to make after all.
and local indian restaurants
just didn't help to fill the void either.
thus i finally accepted that i needed her help.

and i began enjoying the conversations
where i asked for her recipes
and complaining when they still turned out subpar.
now it is those spices that remind me of home,
remind me of my culture and my heritage,
and help me to always stay rooted
to the flavors of being raised as a pakistani man
living in an american society.
i will never again shed my foreign skin,
for a forged american skin.

it is because of this journey
that i spike my chai with spices.
to savor the flavors of life.

|| shukriya ||

i poured my soul into this very moment.
to the one who holds my entire being
with love and care
in the palms of their hands,
thank you.

|| alyees qureshi ||

torn between a traditional pakistani-muslim household
while living in an american society, alyees qureshi
wrote his own story to bridge the gap between these
two worlds. rediscovering the very cultural roots he
burried, alyees found peace in embracing the man that
his journey helped him become. although at times,
staying silent is tempting, alyees believes that
expression paves the way for growth, and thus *masala
chai* was born. as a collection of poems, alyees hopes
that his voice will resonate with those facing similar
struggles and inpsire them to express their own too.

masala chai

is the journey of a flower
from blossoming to indulgence.
its essence brews the most flavorful
and aromatic chai,
for it has not only flourished freely
but has also suffered sorrow.

bloom – love
waves – states
heat – fire
boil – chaos
brew – culture
strain – purify
savor – home

*follow this recipe closely
and savor the flavors of life.*

– alyees qureshi

|| alyees's masala chai recipe ||

ingredients to taste:
authentic black tea, honey, cinnamon, cardamom,
cloves, nutmeg, star anise, black peper, fennel, ginger,
tumeric, and coconut flakes.

brew one part water with ingredients
for ten minutes on medium.

strain.

pour whole milk
until black tea turns
a rich golden brown in color.
steam until malai forms
across the surface.

pour into mugs
and savor the blend of flavors
against the wholesomeness of the milk.

and savor every taste
\as you take on
this journey with me.

49252186R00159

Made in the USA
Columbia, SC
19 January 2019